I0816932

FEATHERED FARM ANIMALS

CHICKENS

by Elizabeth Andrews

Cody Koala

An Imprint of Pop!
popbooksonline.com

Hello! My name is Cody Koala

This book is filled with videos, puzzles, games, and more! Scan the QR codes* while you read, or visit the website below to make this book pop.

popbooksonline.com/chicken

*Scanning QR codes requires a web-enabled smart device with a QR code reader app and a camera.

abdobooks.com

Published by Pop!, a division of ABDO, PO Box 398166, Minneapolis, Minnesota 55439.

Printed in the United States of America, North Mankato, Minnesota.

082025
012026

Cover Photo: Shutterstock Images
Interior Photos: Shutterstock Images
Editors: Tyler Gieseke and Grace Hansen
Series Designer: Julia Line

Library of Congress Control Number: 2025940515

Publisher's Cataloging-in-Publication Data
Names: Andrews, Elizabeth, author.
Title: Chickens / by Elizabeth Andrews
Description: Minneapolis, Minnesota : Pop!, 2026 | Series: Feathered farm animals | Includes online resources and index
Identifiers: ISBN 9781098248536 (lib. bdg.) | ISBN 9781098249052 (ebook)
Subjects: LCSH: Chickens--Juvenile literature. | Poultry--Juvenile literature. | Fowls--Juvenile literature. | Farm animals--Juvenile literature. | Animal husbandry--Juvenile literature.
Classification: DDC 636.50--dc23

Table of Contents

Chapter 1

Meet the Chicken!

Chickens are birds. They live in groups called flocks. Female chickens are called hens. Male chickens are called roosters. Hens **cluck**, and roosters **crow**. They are raised for meat and eggs.

Watch a video here!

Chickens are round and covered in feathers. There are 60 **breeds** of chickens.

Most farm chickens are brown or white, but they can be many colors and patterns.

Chickens can grow up to 2.3 feet (0.7 m) tall. They weigh about 5.7 pounds (2.6 kg). Roosters have brighter feathers and longer tails than hens. A chicken has a comb and wattle on its head.

Chickens are usually too heavy to fly.

comb
beak
wattle
tail
wing
claw

Chapter 2

Life on the Farm

Chickens live on farms. Some live in large buildings with thousands of others. Some live in **coops**. Both kinds of shelter keep chickens warm and safe from **predators**. They like to go outside too.

Learn more here!

Hens begin laying eggs when they are five to six months old. Hens build nests to lay eggs. They can lay up to 300 eggs a year.

Hens lay the most eggs during their first year of life. They lay fewer as they get older.

Chickens are social animals. They like to be with at least three others. There are boss chickens in flocks. These chickens get food and water first. Chickens fight to be the boss.

Chapter 3

What Do They Eat?

Most chickens on farms eat special **feed**. They may also eat grains, grass, fruits, vegetables, and bugs. Chickens need fresh water daily.

Chickens don't have teeth. They swallow their food without chewing.

Explore links here!

Chapter 4

Fluffy Chicks

Baby chickens are called chicks. They hatch from eggs. They use their beaks to break out. When they hatch, they have soft feathers called down.

Complete an activity here!

Mother hens cover their chicks with their wings to keep them safe and warm. Chickens **molt** when they are three to six weeks old. They start growing their adult feathers.

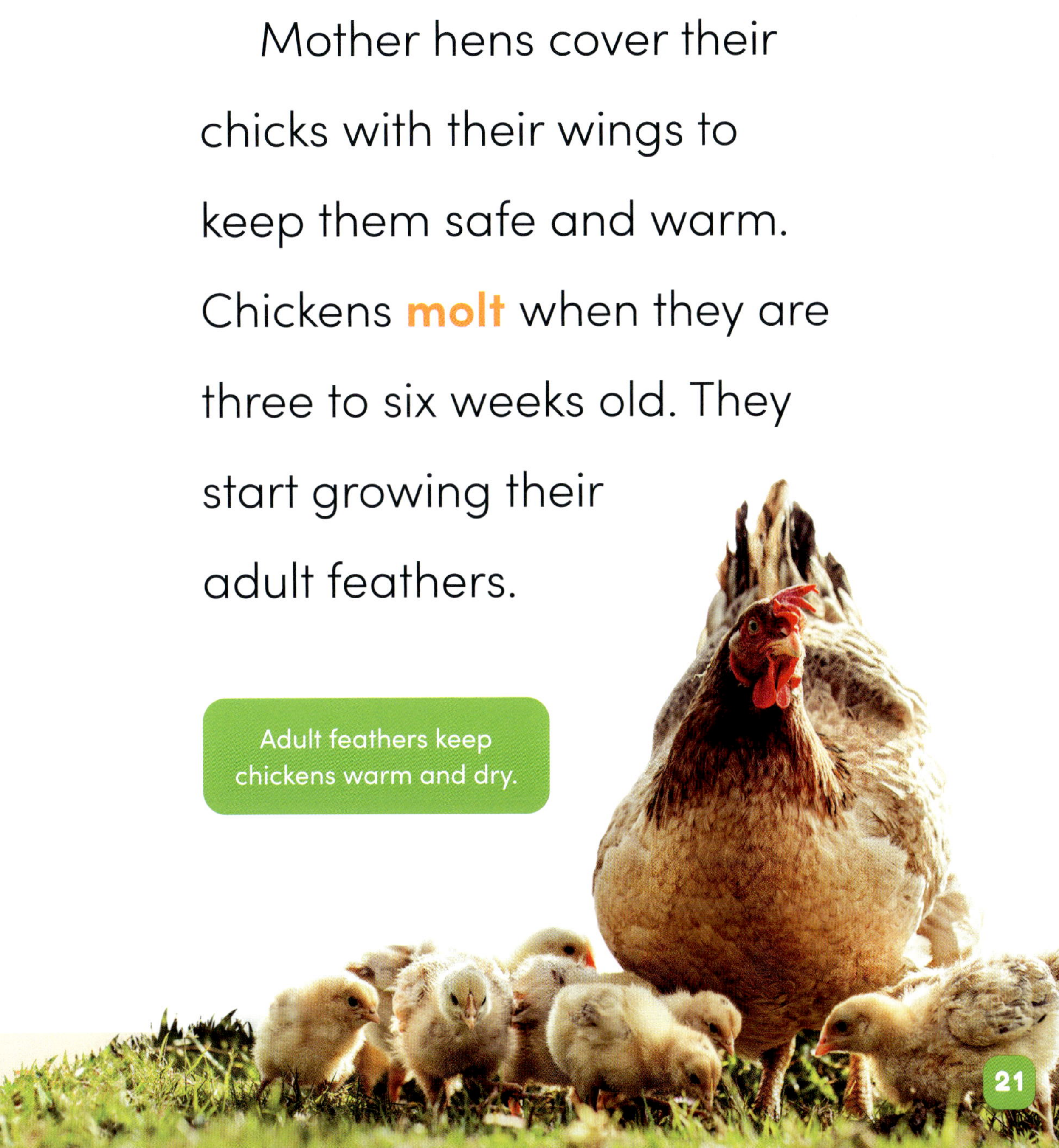

Adult feathers keep chickens warm and dry.

Making Connections

Text-to-Self

What is one new thing you learned about chickens in this book?

Text-to-Text

Have you read any other books about farm animals? How were those animals similar to or different from chickens?

Text-to-World

Chicken is eaten all around the world. With the help of an adult, look up chicken dishes from outside the US. Which dishes would you want to try? Please explain your answer.

Glossary

breed – a specific type of an animal that is raised by humans.

cluck – to make the sound of a hen.

coop – a small enclosed space to house farm birds.

crow – to make the loud sound of a rooster.

feed – food designed for a specific kind of animal.

molt – to have old feathers fall out so new ones can take their place.

predator – an animal that lives by hunting and eating other animals.

Index

Online Resources

popbooksonline.com

Thanks for reading this Cody Koala book!

This book is filled with videos, puzzles, games, and more! Scan the QR codes* while you read, or visit the website below to make this book pop.

popbooksonline.com/chicken

*Scanning QR codes requires a web-enabled smart device with a QR code reader app and a camera.